THE WEAPONS ENCYCLOPÆDIA
TANK AIRCRAFT AFV SHIP ARTILLERY VEHICLES SECRET WEAPON

AF110789

TWE-033 ENG

🇺🇸 SPECIALISED TANKS ON M4 SHERMAN HULL

THE WEAPONS ENCYCLOPAEDIA

EDITORIAL STAFF
Luca Cristini, Paolo Crippa.

ACADEMIC STAFF
Enrico Acerbi, Massimiliano Afiero, Aldo Antonicelli, Ruggero Calò, Luigi Carretta, Flavio Chistè, Anna Cristini, Carlo Cucut, Salvo Fagone, Enrico Finazzer, Arturo Giusti, Björn Huber, Andrea Lombardi, Aymeric Lopez, Marco Lucchetti, Gabriele Malavoglia, Luigi Manes, Giovanni Maressi, Francesco Mattesini, Daniele Notaro, Péter Mujzer, Federico Peirani, Alberto Peruffo, Maurizio Raggi, Andrea Alberto Tallillo, Antonio Tallillo, Roberto Vela, Massimo Zorza.

PUBLISHED BY
Luca Cristini Editore (Soldiershop), via Orio, 35/4 - 24050 Zanica (BG) ITALY.

DISTRIBUTION BY
Soldiershop - www.soldiershop.com, Amazon, Ingram Spark, Berliner Zinnfigurem (D), LaFeltrinelli, Mondadori, Libera Editorial (Spain), Google book (eBook), Kobo, (eBoook), Apple Book (eBook).

PUBLISHING'S NOTES
None of unpublished images or text of our book may be reproduced in any format without the expressed written permission of Luca Cristini Editore (already Soldiershop.com) when not indicate as marked with license creative commons 3.0 or 4.0. Luca Cristini Editore has made every reasonable effort to locate, contact and acknowledge rights holders and to correctly apply terms and conditions to Content. Every effort has been made to trace the copyright of all the photographs. If there are unintentional omissions, please contact the publisher in writing at: info@soldiershop.com, who will correct all subsequent editions.

LICENSES COMMONS
This book may utilize part of material marked with license creative commons 3.0 or 4.0 (CC BY 4.0), (CC BY-ND 4.0), (CC BY-SA 4.0) or (CC0 1.0). We give appropriate attribution credit and indicate if change were made in the acknowledgments field. Our WTW books series utilize only fonts licensed under the SIL Open Font License or other free use license.

CONTRIBUTORS OF THIS VOLUME & ACKNOWLEDGEMENTS
We would like to thank the main contributors to this issue: The profiles of the floats are all by the author. The colouring of the photos is by Anna Cristini. Special thanks to national and/or private institutions such as: Stato Maggiore dell'esercito, Archivio di Stato, Bundesarchiv, Nara, Library of Congress, Wikipedia, USAF, Signal magazine, Cronache di guerra, Fronte di guerra, IWM, Australian War Museum, ecc. A P.Crippa, A.Lopez, Péter Mujzer, L.Manes, C.Cucut, archivi Tallillo. Model Victoria (www.modelvictoria.it) ecc. per avere messo a disposizione immagini o altro dei loro archivi.

For a complete list of Soldiershop titles, or for every information please contact us on our website: www.soldiershop.com or www.cristinieditore.com. E-mail: info@soldiershop.com. Keep up to date on Facebook https://www.facebook.com/soldiershop.publishing

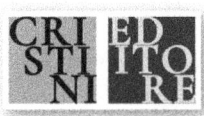

Title: **M4 SHERMAN USA MEDIUM TANK - SPECIALISED VEHICLES VOL. III** Code.: **TWE-033 EN**
Series by: Luca Stefano Cristini
ISBN code: 9791255891703 First edition December 2024
THE WEAPONS ENCYCLOPAEDIA (SOLDIERSHOP) is a trademark of Luca Cristini Editore

THE WEAPONS ENCYCLOPÆDIA
TANK AIRCRAFT AFV SHIP ARTILLERY VEHICLES SECRET WEAPON

M4 SHERMAN USA MEDIUM TANK
SPECIALISED VEHICLES VOL. III

LUCA STEFANO CRISTINI

BOOK SERIES FOR MODELERS & COLLECTORS

CONTENTS

Introduction 5
- Specialised variants for engineers, rescue and other roles 5
- The historical context and the importance of specialised variants 5
- A legacy of ingenuity and versatility 5
- Main conversions list 8

Recovery tanks - genie - antimine 17
- ARV Armoured Recovery Vehicle (M32) 17
- Dozer M1A1 tank 19
- Armoured anti-mine vehicles 25

Amphibious version tanks 35
- M4 Sherman amphibious DD "Duplex Drive" 35
- M4 Sherman amphibious "BARV" 37

Flamethrower, A.A. and rocket launcher 41
- M4 Sherman rocket launcher 42
- M4 Sherman anti-aircraft versions 48

Bibliography 58

▼ An M32 tank recovery vehicle preserved in the tank museum at Fort Knox, Kentucky.

INTRODUCTION

■ **SHERMAN TANKS: SPECIALISED VARIANTS FOR ENGINEER, RESCUE AND OTHER ROLES**

The Sherman tank, officially designated the M4 Sherman, is one of the most iconic vehicles of World War II. Although initially conceived as a medium tank for direct combat, its robustness, reliability and versatility made it the ideal basis for a wide range of specialised variants. In particular, versions designed for military engineering, recovery and auxiliary roles are an outstanding demonstration of engineering innovation and battlefield adaptability.

■ **THE HISTORICAL CONTEXT AND THE IMPORTANCE OF SPECIALISED VARIANTS**

During the Second World War, the Allied armed forces often faced challenges that went far beyond simple tank battles. The need to cross minefields, overcome natural and man-made obstacles, repair damaged vehicles or recover isolated crews required quick and practical solutions. It was in this context that the M4 Sherman established itself as the ideal basic platform for a series of innovative modifications. Thanks to its mass production, compatibility with numerous weapon systems and the simplicity of its mechanics, the Sherman was transformed into a true 'Swiss Army knife', capable of adapting to any requirement.

▲ A British Sherman anti-mine Crab flail tank during testing, belonging to the 79th Armoured Division, 1944.

Specialised variants of the Sherman proved essential in numerous operations, contributing to the success of the Allied forces. Their use became particularly evident during key events such as the Normandy landings, operations in the Italian campaign and the advance across Western Europe. These vehicles were often silent protagonists, operating behind the main lines to ensure that the advance could continue uninterrupted.

■ A LEGACY OF INGENUITY AND VERSATILITY

The Sherman's variants for engineer, rescue and support tasks highlight how modern warfare requires not only destructive power but also adaptability and logistical resilience. Each modification represents a creative response to specific challenges, testifying to the skill of military engineers and the ability of allied troops to make the best use of available resources.

Even after the end of World War II, many of these variants remained in service, continuing to prove useful in later conflicts and peacekeeping contexts. Today, the Sherman and its multiple incarnations continue to be celebrated not only as a symbol of Allied victory, but also as an example of how a single vehicle can embody a multiplicity of roles on the battlefield. This ability to transform and adapt remains a fundamental lesson in the design of modern military vehicles.

▲ A special Sherman BARV vehicle pulls alongside a column of Sherman tanks of the 13th-18th Royal Hussars during the regiment's transfer march from Petworth to Gosport in the summer of 1944.

US Sherman Medium Tank ARV Dozer M1A1 'Apache' version belonging to the 746th Tank Battalion, US Army - Normandy, France, July 1944.

▲ Another profile view of the M32 tank recovery vehicle in the tank museum at Fort Knox, Kentucky.

■ MAIN CONVERSIONS LIST

Below is an initial list of conversions carried out on the Sherman tank. Later on, we will analyse by type all the most well-known and used types of conversions:

ARV armored recovery vehicles

• **M32 Tank Recovery Vehicle**: This recovery vehicle was based on the M4 Sherman. It had a device to lock the tank while the winch was being raised. This was done by means of a telescopic mast so that the towed vehicle remained at a good distance during recovery. The pulling force of this vehicle was 27 tonnes, almost as much as its weight: 28 tonnes;
• **M32B1 tank recovery vehicle**: same vehicle as above but based on the M4A1;
• **M32B2 tank recovery vehicle**: same vehicle as above but based on the M4A2;
• **Tank Recovery Vehicle M32B3**: same vehicle as the previous one but based on the M4A3, with HVSS for the latter;
• **M32B4 tank recovery vehicle**: same vehicle as above but based on the M4A4;
• **M34 Full-Track Prime Mover**: M32B1 without winch used as artillery tractor;
• **M4 Dozer**: M4 equipped with bulldozer blade with or without turrets, for the Corps of Engineers;
• **M4 mobile assault bridge**: bridge installer (2 ramps) equipped with crane (rare);
• **M4 mobile bridge fitters**: installer of British-style bridges of the type: Plymouth with bayley bridge, or Sherman AVRE type with Small Box Girder bridge;
• **M4 Sherman bundle carriers and mobile bridge vehicles**: For overcoming obstacles as ditches and trenches, some Shermans were modified to carry bundles of wood or to serve as mobile bases for bridges;
• **M4 with Cullin Hedgerow Device**: M4s equipped with a frontal blade to pierce and overcome hedges in the Normandy countryside (the bocage);
• **Sherman Observation Post**: a mobile armoured post for artillery control. The cannon was removed (with a dummy barrel mounted on the outside) to make room for the map tables in the turret.

Armoured anti-mine vehicles

- **Mine Exploder T1E1 (Earthworm):** anti-mine tank equipped with armoured discs (rare);
- **Mine Exploder T1E2:** front-equipped anti-mine tank with two 7-disc units (experimental);
- **Mine Exploder T1E3 (M1) "Aunt Jemima":** anti-mine tank equipped with two 5-disc units, used in Italy and Normandy. It sometimes required the thrust of another tank (75 built);
- **Mine Exploder T1E4:** anti-mine tank developed in 1944 equipped with 16 discs in the front;
- **Mine Exploder T1E5:** canti-mine tank based on the T1E3 but with smaller front discs Developed in July 1944;
- **Mine Exploder T1E6:** Mine Exploder tank similar to the T1E3 but with serrated discs (experimental);
- **Mine Exploder T2E1:** anti-mine tank developed for the Marine Corps, used with the M32 tank recovery vehicle by boom. Unsatisfactory and abandoned in October 1944;
- **Mine Exploder T2 Flail:** British-designed anti-mine tank (Crab I);
- **Mine Exploder T3:** anti-mine tank based on the British Scorpion. This version was considered unsatisfactory and development was discontinued in 1943;
- **Mine Exploder T3E1:** T3 anti-mine tank with longer arms and chain rotor. Abandoned like its predecessor;
- **Mine Exploder T3E2:** anti-mine tank based on the T3E1 but with a roller instead of a chain rotor;
- **Mine Exploder T4:** British Crab II anti-mine tank;
- **Mine Exploder T7:** anti-mine tank developed at the end of 1943, equipped with a chassis with small rollers each consisting of 2 discs. Abandoned because it was deemed unsatisfactory;
- **Mine Exploder T8:** an anti-mine tank equipped with steel binders mounted on a pivoting frame. These binders beat the ground at the front of the tank, just like a woodpecker. This tank was difficult to manoeuvre, which earned it the nickname 'Johnnie Walker';
- **Mine Exploder T9:** anti-mine tank equipped with 6 rollers. Difficult to drive;
- **Mine Exploder T9E1:** lighter mine tank than the T9, not very effective because some mines did not explode;

▲ Canadian version of the anti-aircraft vehicle, named Grizzly.

US Sherman medium tank ARV Dozer M1A1 version with metal vents for amphibious operations belonging to the 6th Marine Tank Battalion, Okinawa 1945.

- **Mine Exploder T10:** anti-mine tank equipped with a unit (tricycle) placed under the tank, remotely controlled by the next tank. Difficult to control and eventually abandoned;
- **Mine Exploder T11:** anti-mine tank armed with 6 front mortars (experimental);
- **Mine Exploder T12:** anti-mine tank armed with 23 mortars. This model, although effective, was also abandoned;
- **Mine Exploder T14:** standard M4 tank with reinforced armour and reinforced tracks. Abandoned at the end of the war;
- **Snake Equipment for M4:** standard Sherman tank pushing a snake-shaped explosive charge (used by American infantrymen, particularly during the Normandy landings);
- **Mine Excavator T4:** mine sweeper tank developed in 1942 equipped with a spade. Complicated and therefore abandoned;
- **Mine Excavator T5:** minesweeper tank similar to the T4 but with a V-shaped spade. A modified version was designated T5E1;
- **Mine Excavator T2E2:** Demining tank based on the M4 Dozer with hydraulic arms to lower or raise the blade;
- **Mine Excavator T6:** sdemining tank equipped with a V-shaped spade. Unsatisfactory due to the inability to control the depth;
- **Mine Excavator T5E3:** tank equipped with an angled spade mounted at the front of an M1 Dozer mount.

▲ Sherman transport vehicle throws Twaby Ark bridge with ramps in running position, 4 April 1945.

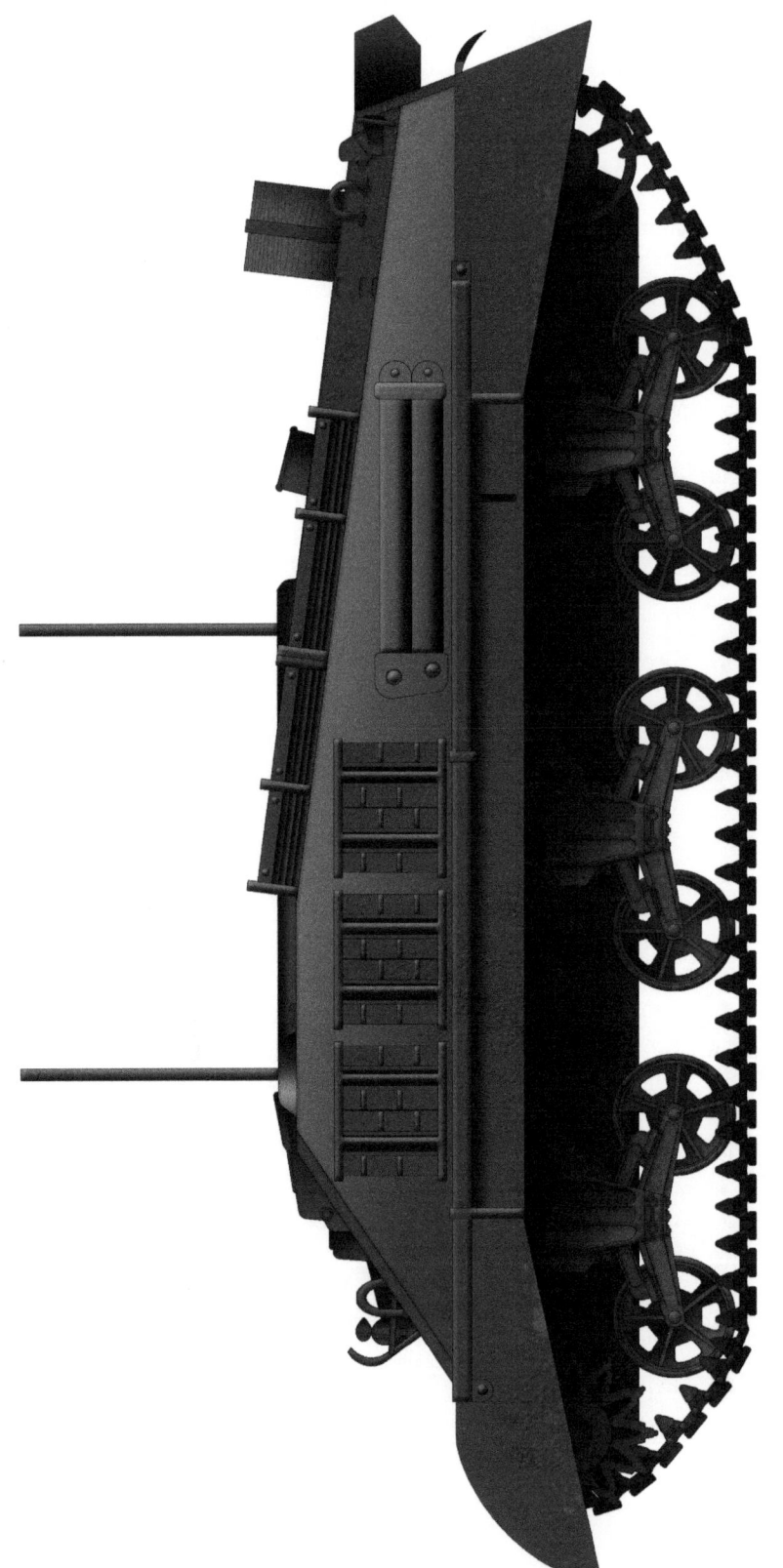

Medium tank UK Sherman V Mark I ARV, belonging to 4th Platoon, 24th Uhlan Regiment, 1944.

▲ Model of an American Sherman minesweeper of type T1E3. Made by the modelling club I Picchiatelli (BG).

UK Sherman M32B1 TRV medium tank in action at Saint-Mère-Eglise, France, June 1944. This recovery vehicle is based on the cast-hull chassis of the M4A1. The version shown here is an early production model.

Flamethrower armoured vehicles

- **E4R2-5R1, E4R3-ER1, (M3-4-3)**: Flamethrower tank: flamethrowers mounted in place of the hull machine gun;
- **E4R4-4R 5-6RC Flame Gun**: flamethrower mounted in place of the hull machine gun. The tanks were installed inside the tank;
- **POA Flame Thrower**: flame-throwing tank whose flame-throwing nozzle was installed in the 105 mm gun tube (US Navy Mk I);
- **POA-CWS 75-H1**: flamethrower tank whose nozzle was installed in the 75 mm gun tube;
- **POA-CWS 75-H2**: flame-throwing tank whose nozzle was installed to the right of the 75 mm cannon;
- **E6-R1 Flame Gun**: flamethrowing tank whose nozzle was installed in place of the hull gunner's periscope;
- **E6-R7 Flame Gun**: flamethrowing tank whose (small) nozzle replaces the cannon;
- **Ronson Flame Gun**: Canadian flamethrower tank;
- **M4 Crocodile**: flamethrowing tank using British Crocodile equipment;
- **Special E1 anti-personnel tank hull**: flamethrowers (4) installed on the body of the tank for close defence against Japanese infantrymen.

Armoured rocket launchers

- **T34 Calliope rocket launcher**: rocket launcher tank equipped with ramps of 60 rocket launcher tubes (100-150 mm), mounted on the turret;
- **T34E1 rocket launcher**: rocket launcher tank equipped with two ramps of 7 rocket launcher tubes, mounted on the turret;
- **T34E2 rocket launcher**: rocket launcher tank equipped with ramps of 60 (long) rocket launcher tubes (182.8 mm), mounted on the turret;
- **T39 rocket launcher**: rocket launcher tank equipped with two apparatuses (with ports) of 20 rocket launchers (182.8 mm), mounted on the (experimental) turret;
- **T40(M17) WhizBang rocket launcher**: rocket launcher tank equipped with two apparatuses (with doors) or frame of 20 tubes (182.8 mm), mounted on the turret;
- **T40 rocket launcher short version**: like its predecessor but with shorter tubes;
- **T72 rocket launcher**: rocket launcher tank equipped with small tubes. Never used;
- **T73 rocket launcher**: rocket launcher tank similar to the T40 but with 10 rocket launchers;
- **T76 rocket launcher**: M4A1 tank equipped with rocket launcher tube (182.8 mm) instead of cannon. Never used;
- **T99 rocket launcher**: rocket launcher tank equipped with two 22-tube (114 mm) turret-mounted apparatuses;
- **T105 rocket launcher**: M4A1 rocket launcher tank equipped with a single-tube housing instead of a cannon.

Armoured vehicles of other types

- **T52 multi-gun tank**: a multi-tank developed by Firestone, armed with 40 mm cannon or one 40 mm cannon and two 12.7 mm machine guns in a rotating turret. Considered too slow, the project was abandoned in October 1944;
- **T31 demolition tank**: M4A3 (105) tank with 182.8 mm rocket launchers mounted on each side of the turret. Never used;
- **M4 Duplex (DD)**: amphibious tank equipped with an inflatable buoy and propelled into the water by propellers. Ineffective, many of them sank during the Normandy landings;
- **M4 Sherman BARV (Beach Armored Recovery Vehicle)**: Designed for amphibious operations, the BARV was used to tow immobilised vehicles in shallow water or on the beach;
- **M4 with amphibious exhaust system**: amphibious tank equipped with air sleeves allowing air flow to the engine and exhaust;
- **T14 tank**: British and Americans tried together to create a super Sherman. The development of this tank was very slow and was never completed before the end of the war in Europe. The tank was too heavy anyway and the Sherman's replacement, the M26 Pershing, was already in production;
- **Sherman Kangaroo**: Canadian tank converted into armoured troop carrier 'Kangaroo'.

▲ A Pakistani Army M32A1 ARV tank now on display in Ayub National Park.

▼ Sherman ARV MK I tank, (Armoured Recovery vehicle), operating in the Caen area. July-August 1944.

RECOVERY TANKS – GENIE – ANTIMINE

Most of the Sherman tanks were converted into tanks for use by the Army Corps of Engineers: recovery tanks, cranes, bulldozers, transport and artillery tractors, the history and characteristics of the best-known among them are given below.

■ ARV ARMOURED RECOVERY VEHICLE (M32)

The M32 tank recovery vehicle, known as the ARV (Armoured Recovery Vehicle), was an armoured vehicle used mainly by the United States during World War II and the subsequent Korean War. Derived from the M4 Sherman medium tank chassis, it was also employed by the British, who received several hundred of them through the Lend-Lease programme in 1944.

The first prototypes, identified as: T5, T5E1, T5E2, T5E3 and T5E4, were completed in January 1943. After various tests at the Aberdeen Proving Grounds, the M32, M32E1, M32E2, M32E3 and M32E4 were approved, although the latter never went into production. There were also versions fitted with horizontal volute spring suspension (HVSS), distinguished by the suffix 'A1' in the model number.

▲ A US Army M32B1A1 recovery vehicle reversing into a ditch after passing a bridge on the road to Hamhung during the Korean War, 1953. Author's colouring.

Sherman ARK (Armored Ramp Carrier) medium tank of the 28th Assault Squadron, 2nd New Zealand Division, April 1945.

SPECIALISED TANKS ON M4 SHERMAN HULL

They entered service in July 1943 and remained active until September 1953 in the US Army. Many more in other armed forces of the following countries: the United Kingdom, Indonesia, Israel, Mexico, Pakistan, Yugoslavia. They participated in all conflicts, from World War II to the Korean War, Suez Crisis, Indo-Pakistani War of 1965, Six Day War, Yom Kippur War

Production began in June 1943 at the Lima Locomotive Works with five pilot cars, followed by various models. Other manufacturers included the Pressed Steel Car Company, the Baldwin Locomotive Works and the Federal Machine and Welder Company. A total of 1,562 examples were produced until May 1945. Some vehicles were converted into M34 Prime Movers for towing heavy artillery.

The M32 was used in Europe from 1944, during Operation Overlord and subsequent campaigns. It was also used in the Korean War, but was gradually replaced by the M74 in 1954 to support more modern and heavier tanks, such as the M46 Patton. The vehicle was equipped with a 27-tonne winch, a 5.5 m boom and an A-shaped arm, with light armament for defence and support during recovery operations.

■ DOZER M1A1 TANK

The experience gained during the Second World War led the US Army to realise the importance of acquiring specialised vehicles for the Engineer Corps, such as armoured bulldozers capable of operating even under enemy fire. Initially, attempts were made to adapt existing commercial vehicles and reinforce them with improvised armour. However, this solution proved insufficient. The protection of these vehicles was too light to withstand intense enemy fire, and the absence of armament made these vehicles incapable of defending themselves independently. So, in January 1942, the first experiments to mount a bulldozer blade on a tank began, but the results were unsatisfactory, mainly due to the design of the blade, derived from commercial models, which was unsuitable for military use. Despite the early failures,

DATA SHEET	
	Sherman ARV M32 USA-UK
Lenght	5920 mm
Width	2700 mm
Height	2940 mm
Date of entry into service/exit	July 1943 until September 1953 (US Army)
Total weight	30 tonnes
Crew	4 (commander, pilot, servants)
Engine	Continental R975 9-cylinder, 350-400 hp radial engine
Maximum speed	39 km/h on road 25 km/h off road
Autonomy	240 km on road, 190 off road
Suspension	Vertical Volute Spring Suspension (VVSS)
Armour	From 13 to 51 mm
Armament	1 81 mm M3 L/40 mortar with 97 rounds 1 Browning M2HB machine gun cal. 50 1 Browning M1919A4 machine gun cal. .30 (7.62 mm)
Production	Over 1,500 until the end of WWII

Sherman fascine carrier medium tank, 28th Assault Squadron, New Zealnd Division, 1944-45.

▲ Sherman ARV Dozer M1A1 formerly belonging to the Italian army and now stored in Bellinzago Novarese (NO).

Sherman V ARV MARK I medium tank with special equipment, 4th Armoured Brigade, Great Britain 1944.

however, the engineers continued to develop the project, working with the Ordance Department and two companies, Le Tourneau and La Plante-Choate. In early 1943, the latter presented two new prototypes. However, even these models suffered from an inefficient blade design, again leading to the failure of the experiments. Consequently, funds for the project were cut in June 1943.

Despite the difficulties, when all seemed lost, the determination of the Engineer and the willingness of the two companies finally made it possible to build two new self-financed prototypes.

These successfully tested models demonstrated performance comparable to that of the standard Caterpillar D8 bulldozer. The result prompted the authorities to standardise a unique model, called the Tank-Mounted Bulldozer M1', later simply 'Dozer'. This new machine combined the best features of the previous prototypes. Nearly 2,000 examples were produced, which proved to be crucial in the course of the war for the removal of obstacles in combat zones.

After the Second World War, some of these vehicles were also acquired by the Italian Army. These vehicles lasted several years in the Italian Armed Forces, and were only replaced in the 1980s, when the Pioneer Leopard arrived in the Corps of Engineers, allowing the army to acquire a new armoured vehicle designed specifically for earthmoving operations.

One of the surviving examples, now considered a rarity, is kept at the open-air museum of the 4th Tank Regiment in Bellinzago Novarese (NO). Another vehicle, without armament, is now part of the collection of the Museo della Motorizzazione in Rome.

Immediately after the Normandy landings, the Dozer equipped with the D8 Caterpillar blade was used extensively in northern France to set up airfields and base camps in wooded areas. Initially also used for clearing impenetrable brambles in the Normandy Bocage, it was later appropriately replaced by Shermans equipped with the Culin Cutter kit, which proved far more effective for this particular task.

▲ Sherman ARV Dozer M1A1 formerly used by the Italian army and now preserved in Bellinzago Novarese (NO). Other details of the bulldozer blade support levers.

British antimine M4 Sherman 'Crab' 1944-1945.

OTHER GENIE VEHICLES

The M4 Doozit was a dozer vehicle based on the M4 Sherman, equipped with demolition charges mounted on a wooden platform. However, unlike the T40 WhizBang, this model was never used in combat.

The M4 Bridgelayer was a variant of the M4 Sherman, developed in several versions by both the United States and Commonwealth countries. First introduced in Italy, this configuration featured a turretless M4 with an assault deck supported by a rear counterweight frame. British variants included the Fascine Crib Carrier, the Twaby Ark, the Octopus used by the 79th Armoured Division, the Plymouth (equipped with a Bailey deck) and the US Sherman AVRE with a Small Box Girder deck.

ARMOURED ANTI-MINE VEHICLES

Mine tanks were equipped with a vehicle-mounted device that made it possible to cross a minefield safely by deliberately detonating mines in front of the transporting vehicle. This type of weapon was first used by the British during the Second World War.
The first British model known as the Crab consisted of a series of heavy chains ending in fist-sized steel balls (flails) connected to a rapidly rotating horizontal rotor mounted on two arms in front of the vehicle. The rotation of the rotor caused the steel end balls to spin wildly and slam violently into the ground. The force of the impact of a flail on a buried mine simulated the weight of a person or vehicle and caused the immediate detonation of the mine, but safely and with little or no damage to the flail or vehicle.

▲ Sherman M74 recovery vehicle. An upgrade of the M32 to provide the same capability as the heavier post-war tanks converted from M4A3 HVSS tanks. In appearance, the M74 is very similar to the M32, equipped with an A-Frame crane, a main towing winch, an auxiliary winch and a manual service winch. The M74 also has a front-mounted spade that can be used as a support or a bulldozer blade.

▲ A Polish Sherman reinforced with sandbags, Cassino area, Italy. May 1944.

▲ Front view of the anti-mine system of the British Sherman Crab.

M4 Sherman antimine T1E3 'Aunt Jemima' USA, service in Europe, 1944-1945.

▲ Top view of the Sherman antimine T1E3 'Aunt Jemima'.

SHERMAN ANTIMINE BRITISH CRAB TYPE

The British, who were at the forefront in this field, developed several experimental tanks equipped with demining flails, including the Scorpion, based on the Valentine tank. But it was those designed for the Sherman that were most successful, such as the Mark V Scorpions and the so-called Sherman Lobster. In the end, the model that came out on top was the Sherman Crab (see profile on page 24).

This was put into large-scale production at the request of Major General Hobart and was immediately deployed in active operations.

The Crab's scourge was powered by the tank's main engine. The Sherman's transmission was modified to include a power take-off, eliminating the need for an external auxiliary engine. The Crab's rotor, which carried 43 flails, rotated at 142 rpm thanks to a drive shaft located on the right side of the tank. To ensure efficient operation even at low speeds, such as uphill, a gearbox was added to regulate the speed of the flail.

A key innovation of the Crab was the integration of blades on the rotor, which cut the barbed wire, preventing the flails from tangling. This solution also made it particularly effective in removing barbed wire obstacles. The initial version of the Crab featured hydraulic arms to adjust the height of the flail, while the improved variant, known as the Mark II Contouring Crab, adopted a system with counterweighted arms that adjusted automatically, ensuring effectiveness even on uneven terrain. A blast shield between the scourge and the tank also offered additional blast protection, while the machine gun in the hull was removed as the scourge and shield blocked its field of vision. The Crab weighed around 32 tonnes, two more than a normal Sherman.

To mark safe routes through the minefields, the Crabs were equipped with canisters of chalk powder that traced the edges of the path. Two lighted spy trees mounted on the rear of the tank allowed the Crabs to maintain formation when operating in a group. However, the dense dust clouds reduced visibility, making careful coordination essential to avoid leaving unmined areas.

▲ An American Sherman antimine T1E3 named 'Aunt Jemima' after a famous flour for making cakes in the shape of giant pancakes!

M4 SHERMAN ANTIMINE T1E3 'AUNT JEMIMA'

In addition to the British, who, as mentioned, were in the vanguard of this type of mine defence, the Americans also drew significant lessons from their experience in the North African theatre. Information gathered by intelligence regarding German coastal and border fortifications in Europe made it clear that the Allied offensive in the north of the continent would have to deal with numerous minefields integrated into the Axis defences. The presence of scattered mines and improvised minefields along the lines of the advance was also expected, particularly during the stabilisation phases of the front.

Consequently, combat training focused on the development of assault techniques capable of quickly overcoming mined areas. Particular attention was paid to the creation of specialised mine clearance equipment, designed to open safe gaps through the controlled explosion of ordnance while resisting enemy fire. Various devices were developed to neutralise concealed mines. As illustrated above, the British favoured the flail system, based on rotating chains. The Americans, on the other hand, adopted devices designed to activate mines through the pressure exerted by mechanical mechanisms such as rollers, pistons, discs or flails. These devices were designed to be robust, effective, and easy to use and maintain.

The most famous model adopted by the US Army was the Mine Exploder T1E3 Aunt Jemima: the Aunt Jemima T1E3 owes its name to the logo of a famous cake mix, because someone thought the large wheels of the explosive resembled giant pancakes.

▲ Another T1E3 deminer, this time mounted on a Sherman ARC recovery vehicle.

▲ Front and back of the Sherman antimine T1E3 Aunt Jemima.

The T1E3 performed well during testing, but proved to be very impractical during operational service. According to one report, to perform a U-turn, for example, a distance equal to three football fields was required! The device destroyed mines well due to its considerable weight, but this also made it quite problematic in terms of mobility, especially in soft terrain where it tended to sink. In these situations, it was often necessary to call in other Sherman tanks to push it out of precarious positions...

The few US units that did employ it were soon overwhelmed by the problems of its manoeuvrability and thus lost all interest in using it. In comparison, the earlier British 'Crab' device, which used rotating chains mounted on a Sherman to neutralise mines, proved far more effective and practical.

▲ Sherman antimine US version T1E3.

DATA SHEET	
	Sherman Antimine T1E3 USA
Lenght	3600 mm
Width	3300 mm
Disc diameter	2400 mm
Date of entry into service/exit	July 1944-1945
Total weight	26 tonnes + 2 tonnes per disc
Crew	4 (commander, pilot, servants)
Producer	Whiting
Maximum speed	4,8 km/h undergoing anti-mine cleaning 16 km/h cruising/displacement
Autonomy	150 km on road, 190 off road
Maximum trench depth	1 m
Production	about 75 but only about 30 operational

▲ More pictures of the American T1E3 anti-mine tank, which give a good idea of the bulkiness of the heavy device attached to the front of the armoured vehicle.

M4 Sherman antimine American T1E3 mounted ARV (armoured recovery vehicle) version - service in Europe, 1944-1945.

AMPHIBIOUS VERSION TANKS

■ M4 SHERMAN AMPHIBIOUS DD 'DUPLEX DRIVE'

The Sherman DD tank, an acronym for *Duplex Drive* and jokingly referred to by the British as 'Tank Donald Duck', was an amphibious vehicle designed by the British during the Second World War. This term refers mainly to the Duplex Drive variant of the M4 Sherman medium tank, which was used by the Western Allied forces during the Normandy landings in June 1944 and in subsequent conflicts. In essence, DD tanks, like our Sherman, were equipped with a special canvas flotation structure that allowed the vehicle to float and navigate on water. Propulsion was by means of propellers specially mounted for amphibious use, while the traditional track drive was reused once the amphibious shields were lowered to operate as standard tanks. It was mainly used by the armies of the United Kingdom, Canada and the United States.

The design was the work of engineer Nicola Straussler, who developed it between 1941 and 1944. In addition to the DD Sherman model, other versions were created, such as the DD Valentine and the DD M-10 Destroyer. The maximum speed of the tank in amphibious mode reached 4 knots (7 km/h).

In combat

The main deployment of the DD tanks took place on D-Day, 6 June 1944. That was the real baptism of fire of these revolutionary vehicles. Later, they were also used in other significant operations, such as Operation Dragoon, the Allied invasion of southern France on 15 August 1944, Operation Plunder, which marked the British crossing of the Rhine on 23 March 1945, and some missions on the Italian front in 1945. A number of these tanks were also sent to India, where the 25th Dragoon Reg-

▲ Sherman DD (Duplex Drive) amphibious tank with waterproof floating screen. In the water, the floating screen was raised and the rear propellers came into operation.

Sherman DD (Duplex Drive) medium tank, with flotation device, belonging to the 10th Canadian Armoured Rgt, Juno Beach, Sector Nan, Normandy, 6 June 1944.

iment was trained in their use, but the planned operations against the Japanese in Malaya were ultimately never realised. During D-Day, the DD Sherman tank was assigned to eight tank battalions of American, British and Canadian forces to support the Normandy landings.

The tanks were transported on Tank Landing Craft (LCTs). Normally, an LCT could carry nine standard Shermans, but the bulkier design of the DDs reduced the capacity: the British and Canadian LCTs could carry five, while the smaller American LCTs with a length of about 37 metres (120 feet) could only carry four. The DD tanks were launched into the sea about 3 kilometres (2 miles) from the coast. From there, they independently 'swam' to the beaches to support the assault on the German defences. However, their performance varied between significant successes and major failures, being most notable for the heavy losses suffered during the assault on Omaha Beach. In fact, on all beaches except the 'Sword' many pieces ended up under water, resulting in the loss of its unfortunate crews in some cases. At Omaha beach, almost all the tanks were lost.

■ M4 SHERMAN AMPHIBIOUS 'BARV'

The Armoured Beach Recovery Vehicle (BARV) was an armoured recovery vehicle used for amphibious landings.

Three different BARVs were made in the service of Great Britain since their introduction during the Second World War. The vehicle was also used by the Dutch and Australian armed forces.

The original BARV was a variant of the Sherman M4A2 tank, modified to make it waterproof.

The original tank turret was of course removed and replaced with an armoured, raised superstructure. About 60 of these specialised vehicles were deployed on the beaches during the Normandy invasion. Designed to operate in waters up to a maximum depth of 2.7 metres, the BARV was mainly used to clear stranded or submerged vehicles obstructing access to the beaches. It was also used to unseal small landing craft and other vehicles stranded on the sand. A special feature of this tank was the presence of a diver among the crew members, who was responsible for attaching tow chains to the trapped vehicles.

The BARV was a vehicle developed and operated by the Royal Electrical and Mechanical Engineers. The Sherman M4A2 was chosen as the basis because its welded hull was considered easier to waterproof than those of other tanks. In addition, the M4A2 was powered by a diesel engine, which was considered more resistant to sudden temperature changes due to regular immersion in cold water. A few Sherman BARVs, which proved to be long-lived, remained in service until 1963, when they were replaced by an updated version based on the Centurion tank.

M4A2 with T6 flotation device, 711th US Army Tank Battalion 1944.

▲ Various pictures of operations with amphibious Sherman, DD and BARV vehicles. One can clearly see the operation of the floating structure, which, however, proved almost unsuccessful in rough seas.

British Armoured Beach Vehicle (BARV), Royal Electrical and Mechanical Engineers (REME), Normandy, June 1944.

US Sherman M4 Crocodile Flamethrower Medium Tank of the 739th Tank Battalion, Germana 1945.

FLAMETHROWER, A.A. AND ROCKET LAUNCHER

■ M4 SHERMAN FLAMETHROWER

The effectiveness demonstrated in combat by the Satan flamethrower tank mounted on the M3A1 light tanks prompted the commanders of the armoured units to request a similar installation on the Sherman M4 medium tanks. For this, the idea was to reuse the barrels of the old 75 mm guns to mount the flamethrower lances. The result was a new tank model, officially named POA-CWS '75' H-1 (where 'H' stood for 'Hawaii'), which was used in battle during operations on the Ryūkyū Islands. Later, the vehicle was used on Okinawa in a special configuration, designed to eliminate Japanese defenders hiding in deep caves.

Both models replaced the main cannon with a flamethrower, a solution not appreciated by the crews, who would have preferred to retain a powerful defensive weapon. Attempts had already been made to install a flamethrower next to the cannon on some Sherman tanks, and in the final stages of experiments, some M4s with 75 mm cannons or 105 mm howitzers were equipped with coaxial flamethrowers. However, the shortage of spare parts prevented the large-scale realisation of these modifications.

Previously, attempts had also been made to mount portable flamethrowers on light tanks, firing through slits in the hull, but with little success. Thus, in October 1943, the chemical service was asked to develop a replaceable flamethrower with a casemate machine gun for the M3, M4 and M5 tanks. As many as 1784 of the M3-4-3 model were produced for the M4.

Many of these were used both in Europe and in the Pacific theatre.

In order to keep the machine gun in the casemate, however, an alternative was devised whereby the gun was mounted on the turret, next to the periscope of the tank leader. This configuration, called the M3-4-E6R3, was developed but did not arrive in time to be used in war.

Once again, it was the troops stationed in Hawaii who independently created additional flamethrowers. Using the M1A1 portable model, they developed a casemate-adaptable version of the M4 Sherman. A

▲ US Crocodile-type Sherman flamethrower with fuel-carrying trolley at the rear. Summer 1944.

total of 176 tanks were converted and deployed in the Iwo Jima and Okinawa campaigns, but their use was limited as troops preferred the 'local' modifications that involved mounting the flamethrower on the turret.

Based on the hard experiences gained by fighters during battles on Japanese Pacific islands, the T33 mechanised flamethrower was developed as a crucial weapon for the planned invasion of Japanese mainland islands. However, the end of the war in the Pacific halted production after only three prototypes.

As evidenced by operations in the Pacific Theatre, the flamethrower proved to be an extremely effective weapon, but its use presented a serious tactical vulnerability: operators had to get very close to targets in order to strike, exposing themselves to enemy fire.

Finally, in the M4 Sherman medium tanks, a configuration coaxial to the main gun was tried out with the T33 model, allowing the vehicle to retain its standard warfare capabilities while adding the functionality of the flamethrower.

Finally, a later flamethrower variant, called the Zippo, was developed by the USMC, which deployed it in Okinawa, in support of the 1st Marine Division, in May 1945 (see profile on page 45).

■ M4 SHERMAN ROCKET LAUNCHER

The T34 (Calliope) weapon system was a tank-mounted multiple rocket launcher system employed by the United States Army during World War II. This launcher was installed on top of a Sherman M4 tank, with clearly visible vertical side frames attached to the sides of the turret. It was designed to fire bursts of 4.5-inch (114 mm) M8 rockets through 60 launch tubes.

A kind of American Katiuscia developed in 1943, it was produced in limited quantities and employed by several US armoured units between 1944 and 1945. The name 'Calliope' was reminiscent of a musical organ, with parallel tubes that resembled the launcher configuration. It was certainly the best known of the rocket launchers designed for the Sherman's hull.

The T34 version of the Calliope system was equipped with a total of 60 rocket tubes, divided into an upper fixed group of 36 tubes and two lower detachable groups of 12 tubes each (24 tubes in total). The

▲ American Sherman type M4A3R2 HVSS Zippo in action on the Japanese island of Jwo Jima, 1945.

Sherman T33 HVSS medium tank. By the end of the war it was considered the most advanced flame-throwing tank in existence.

SPECIALISED TANKS ON M4 SHERMAN HULL

▲ Sherman T33 HVSS medium tank, considered the most advanced flame-throwing tank in existence.

▼ 4.5-inch M4-Sherman 'Calliope' multiple rocket launcher, mounted on the M-4A-3 tank of the US 14th Armoured Division, France 1944.

Sherman M4A3R2 HVSS Zippo medium tank, a variant of the flamethrower developed by the USMC. This vehicle was deployed to Okinawa, in support of the 1st Marine Division, May 1945.

▲ Top view of the American Sherman rocket launcher 'Calliope'.

rockets, with a calibre of 4.5 inches (110 mm) and stabilised by fins, contained high explosives with a power equivalent to that produced by an M101 howitzer. These rockets had a maximum range of between 3.5 and 4 kilometres.

The launcher was connected to the barrel of the 75 mm M2-M6 cannon by an articulated arm attached to the launcher with a swivel joint and to the cannon by a split ring. This particular configuration allowed the rocket launcher to follow the same vertical movement as the cannon, with an elevation and depression angle of between +25 and -12 degrees. The entire structure was supported by a strong support beam bolted to the left and right sides of the turret, positioning the launcher approximately one metre above the turret itself.

The rockets were operated electrically through cables that passed through the tank commander's hatch. However, the rocket launcher installation rendered the main cannon unusable. To overcome this limitation, field crews made modifications to the installation, allowing the cannon to fire at a reduced elevation angle. More advanced versions of the launcher included flame deflectors to prevent rocket exhaust from entering the engine compartment. The Calliope was also improved in two new variants: the T34E1: Similar to the T34, but with 14-tube assemblies instead of the 12-tube detachable assemblies. And the T34E2 version: Based on the T34E1, but with an improved rocket ignition system.

Another model of rocket launcher used by the US Army was the T40/M17 Whizbang Rocket Launcher,

▲ Whizbang type rocket launcher system mounted on an M4A1 Sherman named Arlene III. Italy, 1944.

▲ A Sherman Calliope Rocket Launcher tank belonging to the 3rd Army.

(see profile on p. 53) sometimes also just called the WhizBang. This was an M4 Sherman tank-mounted multiple rocket launcher system used by the US Army during World War II. The vehicle had 20 180 mm launch tubes. It was designed to fire high-explosive T37 rockets or chemically charged T21 rockets. Developed in the final stages of the conflict, the Whizbang had rather limited use between 1944 and 1945. A version with a more compact configuration was also produced. The rocket launcher consisted of a parallelepiped frame containing 20 180 mm launch tubes, arranged in two rows of 10. The entire structure was integrated with the hydraulic system of the main gun of the tank, allowing the rocket launcher to follow the elevation movements of the gun. In addition, the system was designed to be quickly removed, allowing the tank to return to its standard attitude and use the 75 mm cannon. The rockets could be fired one at a time or in salvoes, depending on tactical requirements.

■ M4 SHERMAN ANTI-AIRCRAFT VERSIONS

The best known of the Sherman anti-aircraft guns was the work of the Canadian Army. Named Tank AA, 20 mm Quad, Skink was a self-propelled anti-aircraft gun designed in Canada between 1943 and 1944 at the express request of the First Canadian Army to protect its troops from attacks by the German Luftwaffe. However, production was stopped in 1944 after the construction of only three examples, themselves based on the hull of the Grizzly I, the Canadian Sherman. This decision was made due to the declining air threat posed by the German Luftwaffe during that final phase of the conflict.

The tank mounted a fully enclosed turret equipped with four 20 mm Polsten automatic cannons, capable of firing 650 rounds per minute per gun. The hydraulic system allowed rapid turret rotation of up to 65 degrees per second and cannon elevation between -5° and +80°. The armament was controlled by a joystick and a reflector sight, offering remarkable accuracy. It was, from a technical point of view, a very

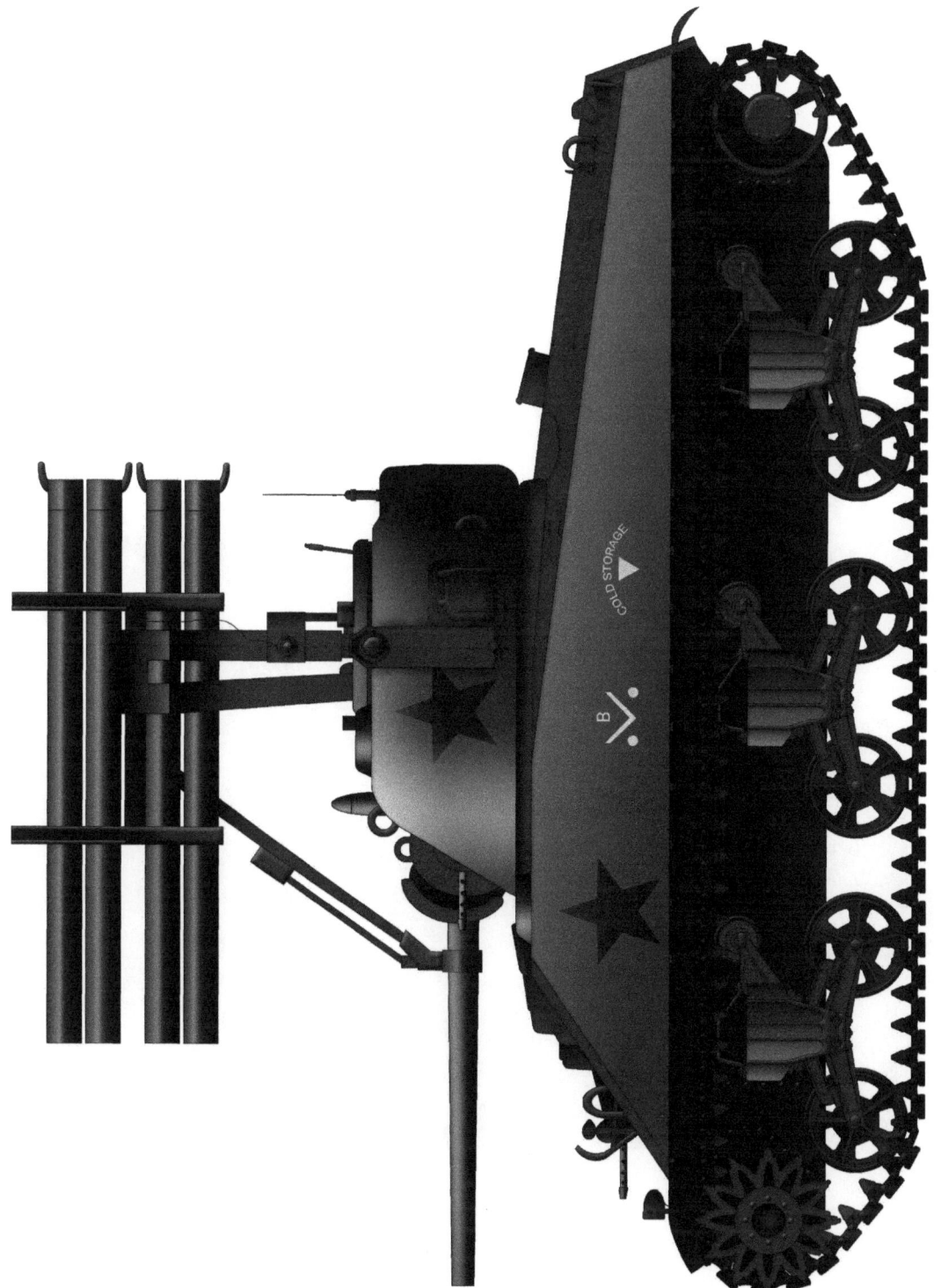

US Sherman M4A3 (75)W 'Calliope' medium tank (T34 Rocket Launcher).

▲ Front view of the American Sherman 'Calliope' rocket launcher.

▲ Rear view of the American Sherman 'Calliope' rocket launcher.

advanced vehicle.

With an operating weight of about 28.5 tonnes, the vehicle was powered by a 350-horsepower Continental R-975C1 radial engine, which gave a top speed of 38.5 km/h and a range of about 193 km.

Despite modern technical innovations, the Skink encountered several problems during testing. The change from Hispano-Suiza to Polsten guns required many modifications to the turret, with complications in ammunition supply. In addition, the 30-round magazines were less practical than the 60-round magazines, while some components, such as the hydraulic system and sights, needed further improvement. Finally, the design of the vehicle exposed the gunner to risk, as he had to lean out of the hatch while firing.

A prototype of the Skink was sent to Europe in 1945 and assigned to the 2nd Canadian Armoured Brigade. Although there was no opportunity to engage enemy aircraft, the vehicle proved effective in infantry support, used to flush out besieged enemy troops. In one incident, a burst from its guns drove 45 German soldiers to surrender, with only 10 wounded. However, the vehicle never faced other tanks and did not have armour-piercing ammunition suitable for anti-tank combat.

Another anti-aircraft vehicle was the T52 project. A second self-propelled anti-aircraft gun based on the Sherman, this time of US inspiration. This was the T52, a Sherman equipped with a rotating turret with two light machine guns in the corners coupled with a 40 mm in a ball turret. Very little information is available on this vehicle, however.

▲ Sherman AA experimental tank, Multiple Gun Motor Carriage T52 1944-45 and model of the same.

US Sherman M4A1 medium tank armed with T40/M17 Whizbang 7.2 rocket launcher, 752nd Battalion, Italy 1944.

▲ The Canadian Sherman anti-aircraft Skink. A modern and futuristic vehicle, however it arrived late in the conflict.

▲ Sherman T52, main US anti-aircraft system design mounted on Sherman hull.

Canadian Sherman 'Skink' AA tank (first model), 1st Canadian Army, Elgin Regiment, Europe, February 1945.

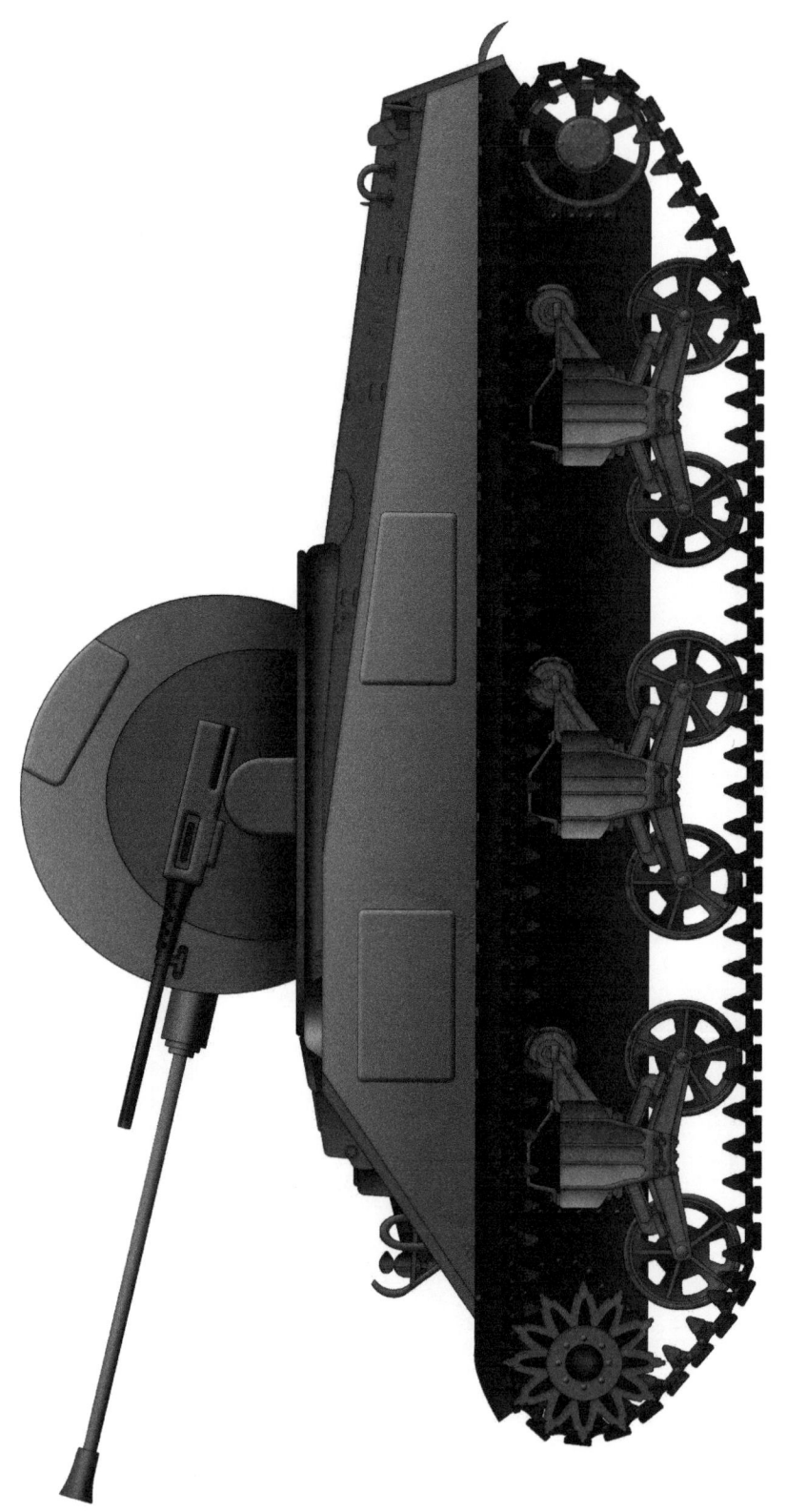

Sherman AA experimental tank, Multiple Gun Motor Carriage T52 1944-45.

M4 tank (latest versions) HVSS with new M26 Pershing turret, 1945-50.

SPECIALISED TANKS ON M4 SHERMAN HULL

BIBLIOGRAPHY

- Bishop, Chris *The Encyclopedia of Weapons of World War II* (2002) Metro Books.
- Calderon e Fernandez, *Sherman the American miracle,* spain 2017
- Chamberlain, Peter; Ellis, Chris. *British and American Tanks of World War II.* New York: Arco.
- Culver B. *"Sherman in Action",* Squadron/Signal Publications, 1977.
- Doyle David, *Sherman Tank, Vol. 6: M32- and M74-Series Sherman-Based Recovery Vehicles*
- Esteve Michel, Sherman: *The M4 Tank in World War II* Casematte pubblisher
- Fletcher D., *"Sherman Firefly"*, Osprey Publishing Ltd., 2008.
- Ford Roger, *The Sherman Tank: Weapons of War* , History press UK
- Forty G. *"United States Tanks of World War II"*, Blandford Press, 1989.
- Gawrych Wojcisch, *M4A2 Sherman Part 1.* Armor photogallery
- Gawrych Wojcisch, *M4 Sherman WC Firefly.* Armor photogallery
- Askew Michael, *M4 Sherman Tanks: The Illustrated History of America's Most Iconic Fighting Vehicles*
- Hunnicutt, R. P. Sherman, *A History of the American Medium Tank.* 1978; Taurus Enterprises.
- Mesko J., *"Walk Around M4 Sherman"*, Squadron/Signal Publications, 2000.
- Mokva Stanislaw, *M4 Sherman: M4, M4A1, M4A4 Firefly,* Kagero
- Oliver Dennis, *British Sherman tanks 1944-1945*
- Oliver Dennis, *British armor in Sicily and Italy 1944-1945*
- Oliver Dennis, *Sherman tanks US army in Europe 1944-1945*
- Porter, David *Allied Tanks of World War II (World's Great Weapons)* (2014) Amber Books
- Sandars J. *"The Sherman Tank in British Service 1942-45"*, Osprey Publishing, 1982.
- Stansell P., Laughlin K., *"Son of Sherman Vol. 1: The Sherman Design and Development"*, The Ampersand Group, 2013.
- USMC D-F Series Tables of Equipment (TOEs), 1942-1944.
- White B. T., *"British Tanks and Fighting Vehicles 1914-1945"* Ian Allan Ltd., 1970.
- War departement, *M4 Sherman Medium Tank Crew Manual*
- Ware Pat, *M4 Sherman: Entwicklung, Technik, Einsatz*
- Ware Pat, *Char Sherman: Toutes les variantes du M4 depuis 1941*
- Green, Michael *American Tanks & AFVs of World War II.* Oxford. p. 310.
- Nash, Mark (27 January 2018). *"Rocket Launcher T34 'Calliope'".* Online Tank Museum.
- Andrew May *DD Sherman Tank Warriors: The 13th/18th Royal Hussars through Dunkirk, D-Day and the Liberation of Europe.* Pen & Sword 2024.
- Luigi Manes *The Sherman medium tank* Witness to War. Soldiershop Pubblishing

ALREADY PUBLISHED TITLES

ALL BOOKS IN THE SERIES ARE PRINTED IN ITALIAN AND ENGLISH

VISIT OUR WEBSITE FOR MORE INFORMATION ON
THE WEAPONS ENCYCLOPAEDIA:
https://soldiershop.com/collane/libri/the-weapons-encyclopaedia/

TWE-033 EN

www.ingramcontent.com/pod-product-compliance
Lightning Source LLC
LaVergne TN
LVHW072122060526
838201LV00068B/4946